A Great Way to LEARN BASS

by Clive Gregory

Written by Clive during the early spring of 1997. All music examples specially composed for the project.

Edited by: Geoff Ellwood

Assistant editor: Joan Gregory

Photographs by: Michael Pearse

Artwork and design: R & C Gregory Publishing Limited

Text and music typeset by R & C Gregory Publishing Limited

Special thanks to: Rubiah Gregory, Peter Wall, Michael Pearse, Graham Mitchell and Ben Cooper, without whom this series of books would never have been possible.

Third edition, published 2001
(last published as "A Step by Step Guide To Everything You Need To Know About Being A Bass Player", ISBN 1 901690 10 5)

Published by
R & C Gregory Publishing Limited

Suite 7, Unit 6, Beckenham Business Centre, Cricket Lane, Kent. BR3 1LB

ISBN 1 901690 09 1

Copyright © 2001 R & C Gregory Publishing Limited
All rights reserved

The contents of this book are protected by copyright
Unauthorised copying, arranging, adapting, recording or public performance is an infringement of
Copyright.

Printed by CS PRINT & DISPLAY LIMITED, Croydon, England.

This book is dedicated to my wife, Rubiah for her unwavering support during this project. Also to my parents for a lifetime of support.

The book is also dedicated to all of my students, past and present without whom this book would not have been possible.

Clive Gregory started teaching Bass in 1980. Over the past twenty years he has taught many hundreds of bass players, from beginners to session players.

As a working professional over 22 years he has played in a great many bands of every conceivable type and has played on TV, TV jingles, radio jingles, and on BBC radio broadcasts.

His considerable knowledge and experience as bass player and dedicated teacher has at last been made available to a wider audience through his books. "A Great Way To Learn Bass" (formerly "ISBN 1 901690 10 5) is part of the Beginners Series for Guitar, Bass, Drums, Keyboards and Saxophone, by R & C Gregory Publishing and is Clive's second book on the subject and is typical of his thorough approach to the subject. It reflects his understanding of the problems faced by beginners - nothing is assumed, everything is patiently explained with the help of photographs, diagrams and examples.

If you wish to progress further than the scope of this book check out Clive's two other books: "Learn Bass From Beginner To Your 1st Band" [ISBN 1 901690 16 4] which is based on this book but comes with a free integral CD full of play-alongs and examples. Or to really get into bass deep; "Clive Gregory's Foundation Course For Bass Guitar", widely acclaimed and used by many teachers in the UK [ISBN 1 901690 20 2].

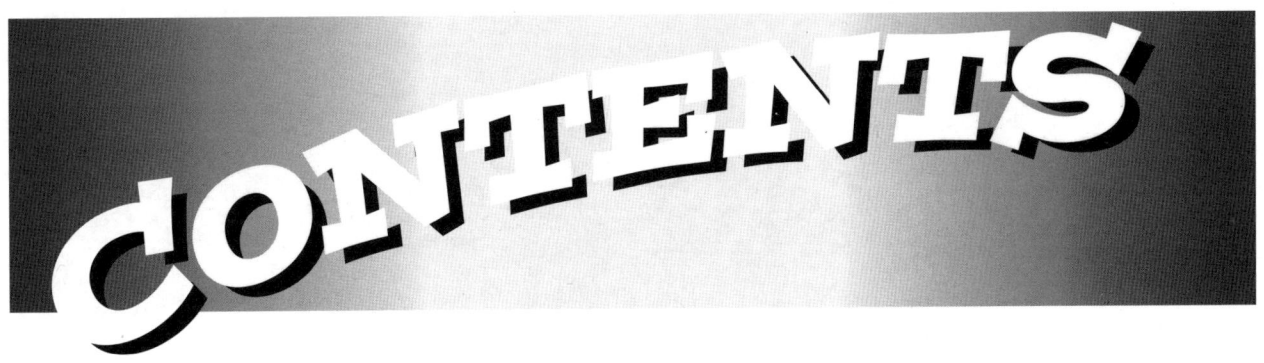

Credits	Page i
Dedications	Page ii
About the Author	Page ii
Index	Page iii
Introduction	Page iv
Your First Time - Getting To Know Your Bass	Page 1
Tuning The Bass	Page 2
The Strap, Posture - Main technique photograph	Page 3
Understanding the notation examples - tab, pictorial	Page 4
Understanding standard music notation	Page 5
Left hand technique	Page 6
Left hand exercises	Page 7
Right hand technique - fingerstyle	Page 8
Pick (Plectrum) technique	Page 9
Living Together - The First Week	Page 10
Getting to know the notes	Page 10
Fingerboard chart	Page 11
Rhythm and time-keeping (rhythm notation)	Page 12
Practise counting	Page 13
The power of silence (rests)	Page 14
Scales and Keys	Page 15
Scales - examples	Page 16
Putting scales into practise	Page 17
Settling Down - Looking To The Future	Page 18
Groove and feel - your real priorities	Page 18
Volume control / tone control	Page 19
Chords and how to deal with them	Page 20
Keys and how to recognise them	Page 21
The 12 bar blues sequence	Page 22
Use of one bar repeating sequences	Page 23
The 7 Week Itch - Getting Into A Band	Page 24
Know your fellow musicians	Page 24
Writing a bass line	Page 26
Outline of improvisation	Page 27
Writing bass line examples / improvisation examples	Page 28
Showing Off - The Art Of Performance	Page 29
Gigging	Page 29
Recording	Page 30
Slap style - technique	Page 30
Are You Serious - Some Stuff To Keep You Going	Page 31
Riffs one and two	Page 31
Riff 3	Page 31
Triple time (triplets) rhythm practise and riffs	Page 32
Sixteenth note introduction	Page 33
Slap style mega riff	Page 33
Additional technique exercises	Page 34

INTRODUCTION

Congratulations on deciding to take up Bass Guitar. This is without doubt the best instrument you could have chosen. The powerhouse of any band. This book is designed for total beginners. To get you started on the road to good bass playing. Playing bass well has as much to do with having the right attitude and understanding your role as a bass player as it has to do with practising or rehearsing with a band.

As well as showing you the basics of technique and helping you to understand how music is put together, this book will try and ensure that when you're good enough to be in a band you understand the musicians around you. There are even tips on how to perform live, how to handle the pressure of the studio etc..

This book is specifically intended to be easy to use, to enable you to quickly get on with the business of playing bass. If you want real in-depth information where no stone is left unturned, I recommend that you buy "Clive Gregory's Foundation Course For Bass Guitar" - available in all good music stores.

So what do you need to know to become a good bass player?

1. Technique: The mechanics of finger movement. This book will outline what is important and useful in developing technique and will give you a few great exercises that will develop your hands and last a lifetime.

2. Musicianship: You need to become a musician and need to understand how music is put together to function as a useful (and therefore popular) bass player.

3. Composition and Improvisation: Most bass players prefer to write their own bass lines - this book will outline how this is done. All good bass players play with freedom. This means that they react to other musicians and even the audience in the way they play and deliver their bass lines. This varies from subtle adjustments to their regular part to full blown improvisation where there is very little in the bass line that is pre-composed.

4. Working with others: This book will try and give you some idea about the musicians you will work with. Also there will be tips about how to cope with live and studio playing - what others will expect of you.

5. Understanding the role of the Bass Player: Probably the best thing that you can get from this book is to really understand what it is to be a bass player. You need the right attitude and priorities if you want to be in the best bands.

Your First Time: Getting To Know Your Bass

Let's assume that you've just bought your first bass and it's on the floor - still in its cardboard box.

I recommend you keep the box as you'll need somewhere to live when you turn pro.

Carefully unpack your new bass. You'll see that there are 4 strings attached to pegs (machine heads) at one end and a bit of metal (the bridge / tailpiece) at the other end. There will be one or two pickups in

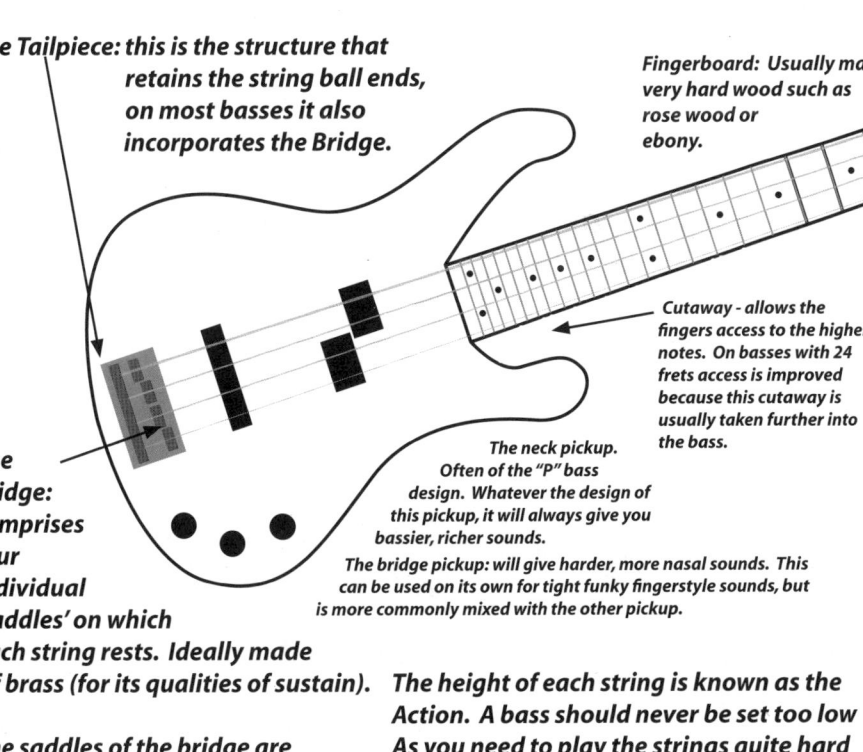

Machine Heads = tuning pegs (sometimes there may be two on each side)

The Tailpiece: this is the structure that retains the string ball ends, on most basses it also incorporates the Bridge.

Fingerboard: Usually made of a very hard wood such as rose wood or ebony.

Neck

Headstock

The Nut; the strings are seated in grooves set into the nut. Usually made of plastic, bone or preferably; brass.

Cutaway - allows the fingers access to the higher notes. On basses with 24 frets access is improved because this cutaway is usually taken further into the bass.

The neck pickup. Often of the "P" bass design. Whatever the design of this pickup, it will always give you bassier, richer sounds.

The bridge pickup: will give harder, more nasal sounds. This can be used on its own for tight funky fingerstyle sounds, but is more commonly mixed with the other pickup.

The Bridge: comprises four individual 'saddles' on which each string rests. Ideally made of brass (for its qualities of sustain).

The saddles of the bridge are adjustable forward and backward and for height.

The height of each string is known as the Action. A bass should never be set too low As you need to play the strings quite hard And buzzing of the strings on frets is not usually desirable.

The electrics on basses differ greatly from bass to bass. One of the commonest arrangements is with 3 controls and two pickups. Usually the first rotary control is master volume. The second is tone - on passive (non powered) basses tone controls are simply high frequency filters. Full off and the filter is doing nothing, full on and the maximum number of high frequencies are filtered out, giving the impression of bassy tone.

Active basses are so called because the electrics are powered, usually by battery. This enables the design to be taken to extremes. Do take care if buying an active bass the circuit is not noisy. There is no point having a wide range of sounds if the hiss created by the circuit is unbearable. A typical arrangement, such as found on the Status 2000 is to have a master volume control, a pickup mix control and a bass cut and boost control and a treble cut and boost control. This provides a very wide range of sounds that are easy to find. Some manufacturers have very powerful circuits, but these usually take a lot of setting up and learning.

the middle of the body under the strings, these convert the acoustic sound into electrical impulses. These impulses are sent, via a few controls out of the bass's jack socket through the lead to the amplifier - you did remember to buy an amp? If not you may get away with plugging into the mic. Socket on your cassette player, putting a tape on record / pause and gradually turning up the volume from **zero** until it is loud enough to hear yourself play. It's not a good idea to have the volume up too high when doing this. Don't play if the speakers are permanently distorted.

Tuning the bass

If you're lucky the bass will have been in tune when it left the shop and should still be in tune when you get home. If you didn't buy an electronic tuner then you should at least buy a tuning fork (costs about £5.00) as you need a starting point to tune from. If you can't wait till the shop opens then you'll have to hope that it's not too far out of tune.

You should always be careful about tuning. Nothing sounds worse than a musical instrument that's out of tune. Play the thinnest string (this is the 'G' string). It should have exactly the same pitch - be perfectly in tune with - the note played on the 5th fret of the string next to it. First of all play the open G string and listen carefully, it's a good idea to try and hum or sing the note. Stop this note from ringing and play the note on the string next to it while pressing down on the 5th fret. Sing or hum this note. You should, even if you're new to music, be able to tell if this second note is higher or lower if the notes are a long way apart, or very out of tune. If you can't hear any difference try playing both notes at the same time. If the combined note sounds like one pure note then these two strings are in tune. If on the other hand there is a wobble or pulsing sound produced by playing both notes together, then you need to tune the second note. Try tightening it, little by little. Listen to the result. Has the wobble got faster or slower. If it has got worse (faster) then you turned the peg the wrong way, if it got slower then you are going in the right direction. Keep going until the sound is completely pure and still - this means the two strings are in tune with each other.

Repeat this for each pair of strings and hopefully you'll be in tune.

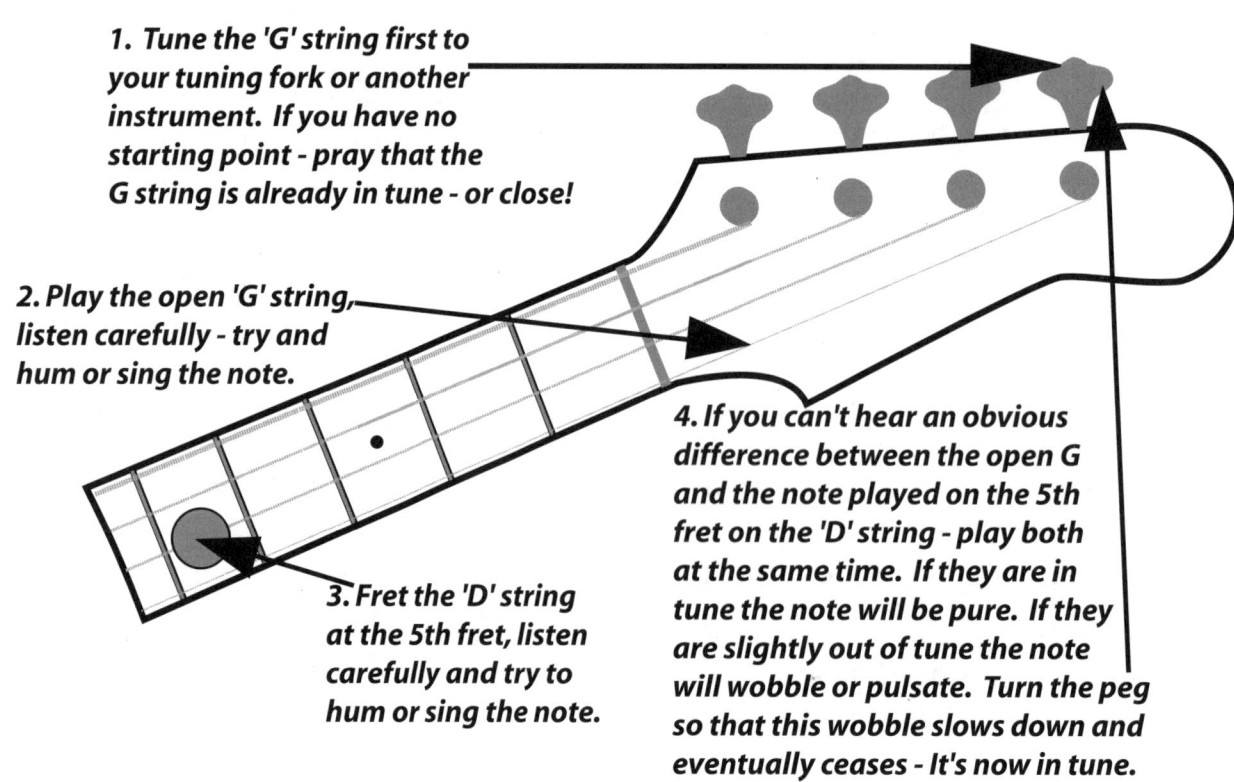

1. Tune the 'G' string first to your tuning fork or another instrument. If you have no starting point - pray that the G string is already in tune - or close!

2. Play the open 'G' string, listen carefully - try and hum or sing the note.

3. Fret the 'D' string at the 5th fret, listen carefully and try to hum or sing the note.

4. If you can't hear an obvious difference between the open G and the note played on the 5th fret on the 'D' string - play both at the same time. If they are in tune the note will be pure. If they are slightly out of tune the note will wobble or pulsate. Turn the peg so that this wobble slows down and eventually ceases - It's now in tune.

It is advisable to buy an electronic tuner as getting it exactly right when you have never played bass before is not always as easy as it sounds. If you have real problems then take it back to the shop and they should be quite happy to tune it for you.

the strap

Firstly, I hope that you bought one as it's a vital piece of equipment. You use the strap standing *and* sitting and height should be set so that it supports the bass in both cases. Ideally, you should try and set the strap so that the bass is in the same position on the chest whether you are standing or sitting.

posture

Your back should be straight at all times. The shoulders should be straight. The shoulders and upper arms support the weight of the hands and arms at all times. Don't lean on the bass with either hand. The bass should be set so that as you bring your left arm up to the neck the forearm is pointing upwards very slightly.

see photo

The right arm shouldn't rest on the bass, although the arm position should be relaxed and so is close to the body of the guitar. However, you may find that your bass lacks perfect balance and therefore you may have to compromise by resting the arm on the body of the bass to stabilise it.

Work on developing an EQUAL stretch between the fingers. Contact the strings with the fingertips (where the bone is will give the best connection), curving all the joints of all the fingers and press the string down just behind the fret you're trying to play. (More about this on page 6.)

Always try and keep the elbow away from the body. The arm position should be relaxed, as if you have raised your hand from your side, bending at the elbow.

understanding the notation and examples

In this book I use as many as three forms of notation. The best way to convey information about music is through the use of standard music notation. Your goal should be to only need this type of notation by the end of this book. However, it's not my intention to force you to read music and it does take some getting used to, although I must stress that it is not difficult. So, in addition to standard music notation I am using tablature (tab) and in some case pictorial diagrams both as an alternative and for greater clarity. You will encounter notation first when learning scales. Compare all three forms and work towards a full understanding of correct music notation. - you know it makes sense...

tab

The principle of tab is that there are four lines drawn across the page. Each line represents a string on the bass. The bass string (E), is at the bottom and the 'G' string at the top. Marked onto these lines are numbers. These numbers are fret numbers.

So Tab illustrates WHICH FRET to play on WHICH STRING.

(Fig. 1 and Fig. 2 relate to the other forms of notation used so that you can easily compare the notation examples.)

fig. 1
How every other note A-C-E-G (the 'SPACES' on the music staff) look in TAB form

A   C   E   G

fig. 2
How every other note G-B-D-F-A (the 'LINES' on the music staff) look in TAB form

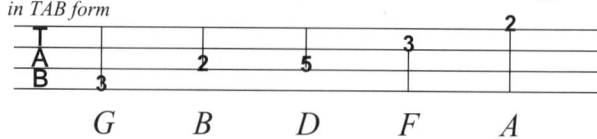

G   B   D   F   A

THE LOW NOTES : See 'clear' notes on fingerboard chart page 11.

LOW E F G A B C D

THE MID. NOTES : See 'light shaded' notes on fingerboard chart page 11

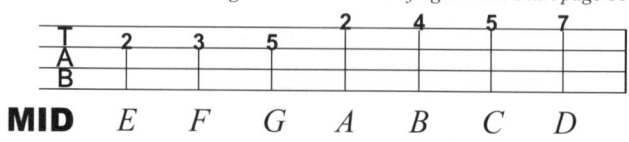

MID E F G A B C D

THE HIGH NOTES : See 'dark shaded' notes on fingerboard chart page 11

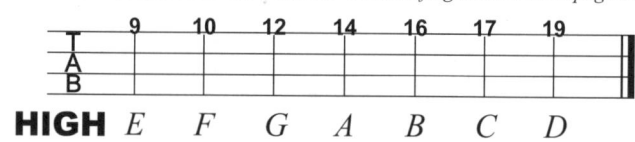

HIGH E F G A B C D

pictorial

The pictorial examples are used to make it absolutely clear where to place your fingers on the fingerboard.

THE NUMBERS INDICATE THE ORDER IN WHICH YOU PLAY NOTES

(See the tab or music examples to find which left hand finger plays the notes - written under the tab or music).

The pictorial examples show where on the fingerboard to play the notes and in which order.

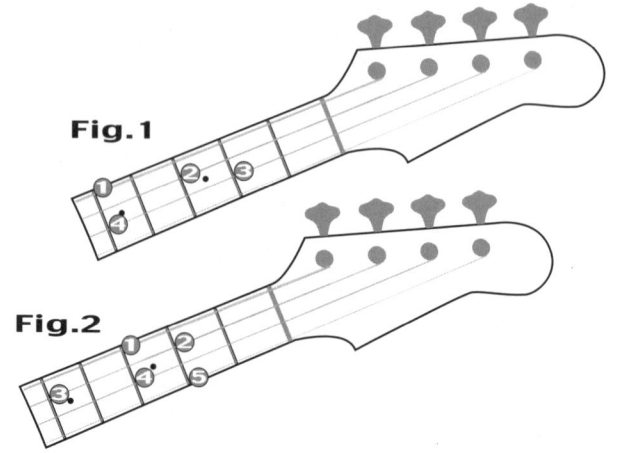

music notation

Standard music notation is perceived as difficult by non-musicians. Understanding written music and learning bass lines etc. is actually quite easy. Reading at sight - immediately playing a piece of music that you've never seen before does require serious study, but need not concern you unless you want to work professionally.

There are five lines drawn across the page. Unlike tab these lines have nothing to do with the strings of a bass or guitar. They are simply a 'grid', called a STAFF (plural - Stave). When we look at a staff we see lines and spaces. Both lines and spaces are used to indicate the pitch (name) of a note.

An effective method for learning the notes is to learn the names of the spaces: A-C-E-G - Fig. 1, and the lines: G-B-D-F-A; Fig. 2.

The beauty of music notation above other alternatives is, that once you're over the basics, you can look at the music and imagine the sound, long before your ear has been trained to do this with 100% accuracy. You can see the melody rise and fall and it is easy to see whether the rhythm is simple or busy, on the beat or heavily syncopated (off the beat).

Rhythm notation is dealt with a little later and is the same for both tablature and standard music notation.

In order to 'activate' a staff a 'clef' is needed. (A French word for key.) There are different types of clef but as bass players we only need learn the Bass Clef. This symbol is also known as the 'F' clef, as it positions where the note 'F' is placed on the 'grid' or staff.

The Bass Clef

Known as the F Clef as it positions the note F on the staff.

Once the clef is in place, all other notes take up their relative positions. Each line or space represents a different letter of the musical alphabet. So the space above the 'F' line, marked by the clef, is the note 'G', and the space below the 'F' line is 'E'.

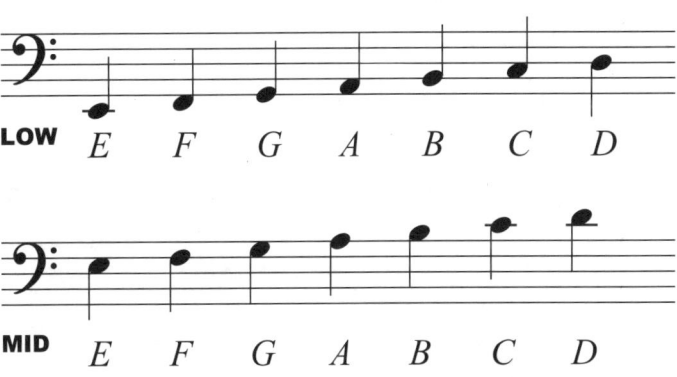

Below are the high notes (see DARK shaded area on fingerboard chart, or above (towards you) the 12th fret on the D and G strings). As these notes are positioned above the staff, LEGER LINES are used to 'continue' the staff. (These high notes are less commonly used.)

left hand technique

Firstly, the thumb. Place it on the back of the neck, more or less in the centre. The thumb is not supposed to be used to squeeze the fingers onto the neck but should enable them to balance and position themselves on the correct string. To make changing strings easy the thumb pivots, or rolls on the ball of the thumb. If you put the thumb in position and place the fingers roughly over the strings you can practise pivoting from string to string. The arm should move freely forward when playing the bass strings with the wrist curved. Move the arm back to play the thinner strings so that the elbow moves behind you and the curve of the wrist is much more relaxed.

The aim of the left hand is to be able to reach as many notes as possible, without moving the hand. Eventually, you will probably want to play as fast as possible, and you will certainly want to play without too much string noise and other unwanted sounds. To do this you need to work on an equal stretch between the fingers. You will need to develop all four fingers so that they are equals in strength and mobility.

For the fingers to be good at their job, they need to play with as little force as possible. You should always try to find your lightest touch. To do this the fingers need to touch the string in the right way, that is using the tips of the fingers, or the boniest part of the finger. They need to press the string down just behind the fret. If you play with either the fleshy part of the finger or press down mid way between frets then you'll end up pressing much harder than is necessary.

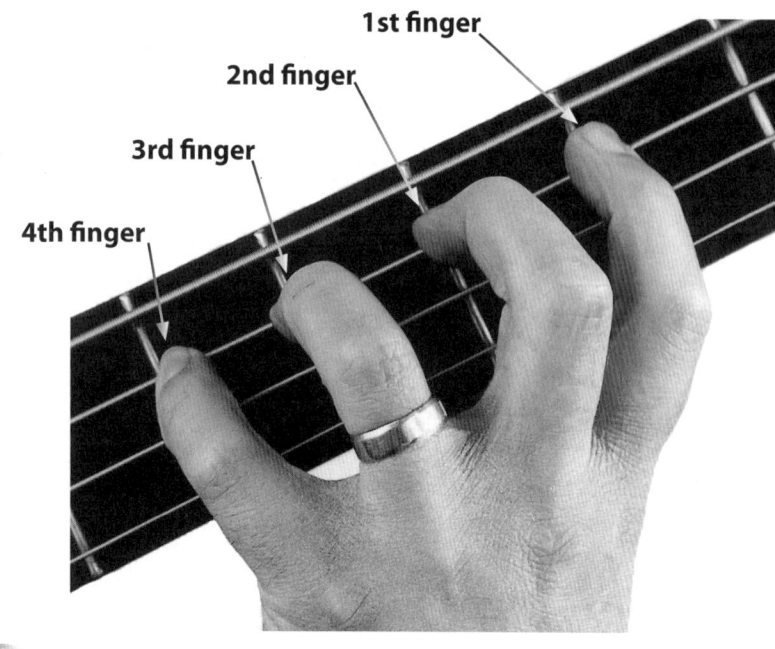

left hand exercises

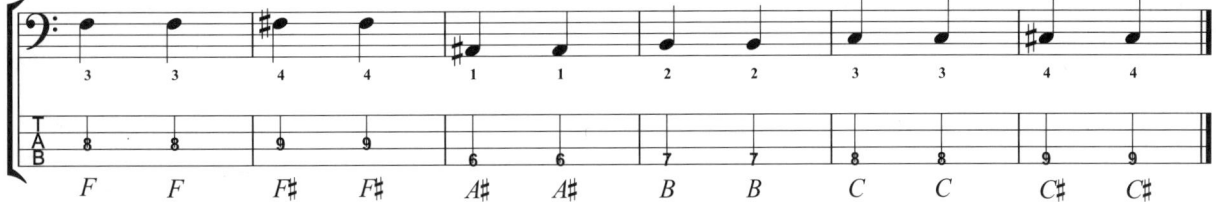

slow stretch exercise

Play each note 4 times at first. When you reach the end of notated section, repeat from the E string back to the starting point.

When it feels easy with 4 notes on each, increase to 8 and eventually to 16 notes. Over a period of weeks choose a position nearer the nut to begin from, until you can start from the 1st fret.

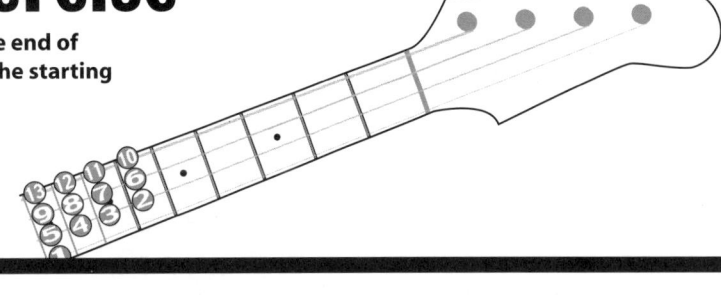

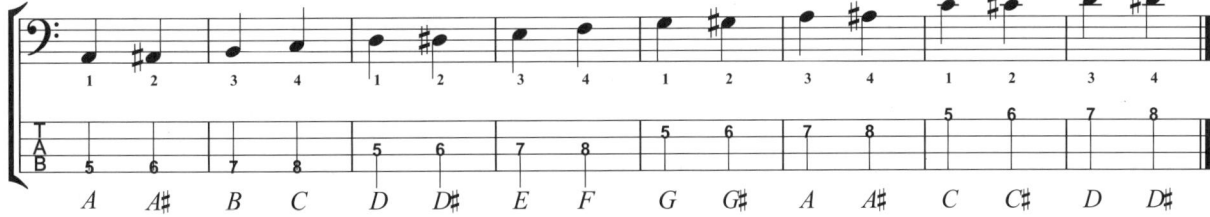

continuous 1-2-3-4 exercise

Play each note once. When you reach the end of the notated section shift the hand one fret towards you and repeat the process. Work from (at least) 6th position (1st finger on 6th fret) to 10th position (1st finger on 10th fret).

When you are used to the exercise keep it going for longer and get faster, so developing stamina.

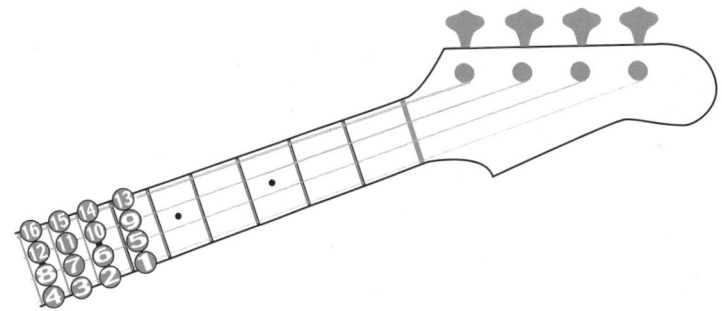

right hand technique

The index and middle fingers of the right hand alternating is the commonest right hand technique. Play very firmly so that you can hear each note attack. Look at the photo to the right to see the angle to hold your hand, also notice that each string is played in a slightly different place, see photos 1-4. This is so that the tone matches from string to string. Unfortunately, playing the bass string nearest the bridge and the G string in the middle of the playing area is not, at first, very natural, but it is worth trying to master this.

1.

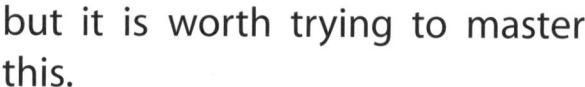

Try not to rest the arm on the bass, support the weight of the arm from the shoulder. The thumb acts as a shock absorber, rather than a rest.

2.

3.

The fingers should squeeze the notes, practise this touch by first resting against the string, build up some pressure and push through. The finger should come to rest on the next string. This is useful as it acts as a buffer, controlling the force in the finger and it will damp, or prevent from ringing, the string it comes to rest on.

4.

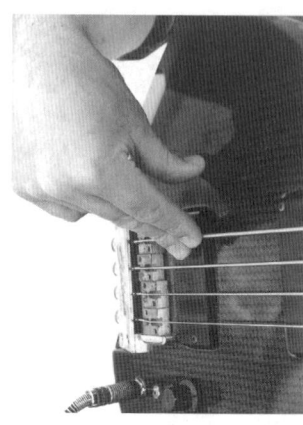

You need to play very firmly. Listen to every note you play to ensure that it has a positive attack. Most good bass players do not realise how hard they play but you can always hear it in the sound.

Playing firmly will also ensure that you develop a good tone and a sound that can be easily modified electronically for an even greater range of sounds.

Although you should generally play on the part of the string illustrated in the photographs on the previous page: about 3-4 inches from the bridge on the 'G' string, to about 1-2 inches from the bridge on the 'E' string. All parts of the string can be used. You will quickly realise that a bassy, warm sound is possible playing near to the neck and tight, nasal sounds are found near the bridge.

You can also experiment with the force you use to play the string with, and with the finger angle etc.

Experiment with sound. Bass players have developed all sorts of different methods for striking the strings.

These 'bracket' signs are repeat signs; repeat everything in between

Practise each string slowly and steadily for about 30 seconds. Use alternate fingers or up and down strokes with the pick.

G STRING   **D STRING**   **A STRING**   **E STRING**

pick (or plectrum) style

The common alternative to playing finger-style is to use the pick (or plectrum). Often students of bass try finger-style and are frustrated by the lack of punch or attack they can achieve. Often they don't realise that it is simply a question of playing harder.

The attraction of the pick is that it always has attack, always has punch and brightness and is often chosen for this reason.

I always recommend getting finger-style down first and learning the pick later, however, it's up to you - which sound do you prefer.

Try and play firmly with the pick also, because although you always have attack, without firmness the sound will be thin and lack bottom end (bass).

slap style (see pages 30 & 33)

LIVING TOGETHER THE FIRST WEEK

getting to know the notes

Learning where to find your notes on the fingerboard is central to communication with other musicians. Really try and learn thoroughly, you need to know every note without conscious thought in order to function as a quality musician.

The musical alphabet uses the first seven letters of the alphabet. This is because in music you normally only use a set of seven notes at any one time.

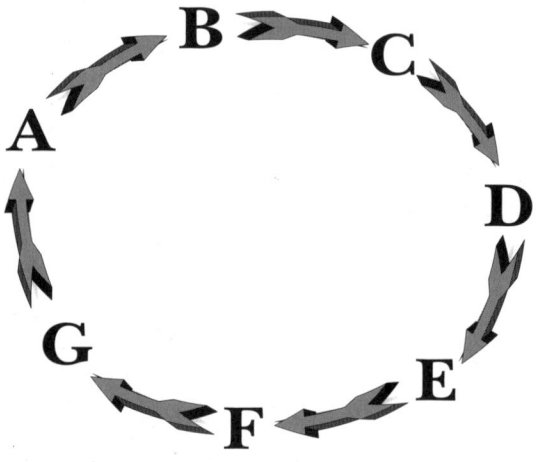

This set of notes is known as the key (more later). As the diagram above illustrates, the seven notes are used cyclically. In other words when you need an eighth note you simply repeat from your original starting point.

When the letters of the alphabet are used on their own, they are known as natural notes. So 'A', is properly known as 'A natural'. Normally musicians can't be bothered to say "natural", so the word is only used if it's necessary to distinguish it from 'A sharp' or 'A flat' (don't panic - sharps and flats explained in a moment).

The distance between one note and the next is not always the same. The distance between notes is referred to as an interval.

The interval between most natural notes is called a 'tone' [In the USA this is called a whole step]. This is equal to 2 frets on the bass. However, the interval from B to C and from E to F is only 1 fret, this interval is called a 'semitone' [USA; half step].

Now learn the open strings: E - A - D - G.

Practise finding each natural note on every string in turn. (Don't actually try and play - just point at the fret and name.) The only knowledge you need for this is to understand the interval or distance between each natural note.

To remind you; they are all a tone (2 frets) apart, except for B to C and E to F, which are a semitone (1 fret) apart. Practise getting to know each string in turn working from the open string, natural note by natural note (E, F, G etc.), until you can go can go no higher. This exercise not only helps you get started on learning the fingerboard, but also reinforces your understanding of how musical notes fit together. Remember this is the same for all instruments.

Don't worry about the sharp and flat notes for now. All you need to know about these is that every letter of the alphabet can have the names sharp and flat applied to them. The sharp note is always a semitone (1 fret) higher in pitch - that means towards you on the fingerboard. The flat is a semitone lower, or away from you towards the head stock.

Next, begin learning how the notes fit together going across the fingerboard. You've already begun this process by learning your open strings.

Pick at first only on those places on the neck where you see 4 natural notes going across the neck such as the 7th fret:

B - E - A - D.

One of these points is the 12th fret. You'll soon realise that these notes match your open strings; the cycle of note names now repeats - these are the eighth notes in sequence and these eighth notes are referred to as the OCTAVE.

	4th String	3rd String	2nd String	1st String
open	E	A	D	G
	F	A#/Bb	D#/Eb	G#/Ab
	F#/Gb	B	E	A
3rd	G	C	F	A#/Bb
	G#/Ab	C#/Db	F#/Gb	B
5th	A	D	G	C
	A#/Bb	D#/Eb	G#/Ab	C#/Db
7th	B	E	A	D
	C	F	A#/Bb	D#/Eb
9th	C#/Db	F#/Gb	B	E
	D	G	C	F
	D#/Eb	G#/Ab	C#/Db	F#/Gb
12th	E	A	D	G

Register
LOW
MID
HIGH

rhythm and time-keeping

Time-keeping is your most important function. You need to become obsessed with this whole area of your playing.

Getting good at rhythm and time-keeping involves a lot of repetitive practise.

Accuracy and consistency are vital if you are to succeed in these areas.

It is useful to introduce you to some music notation at this point. Rhythms are made up from arithmetically related elements. In other words; you have notes that last (sustain) for 4 beats, 2 beats, 1 beat, half a beat etc.. Each of these elements has a name and a symbol. Learning the symbols is quite easy because there are only 5 or 6 that you need to remember.

Rhythm can become quite complex if the basic elements are mixed together. The most complex rhythms arise when a rhythm element is played off the beat (in the middle of two beats, or on any arithmetic division of the beat).

Playing off the beat is known as syncopation and will be dealt with a little later in this book.

For now you need to become familiar with the basic elements.

THE DIAGRAM ON THE RIGHT SHOWS YOU HOW THE RHYTHM ELEMENTS LOOK AND HOW THEY ARE COUNTED:

1. The whole note

o

1 & 2 & 3 & 4 &

sustains for 4 beats.

2. The half note

1 & 2 & 3 & 4 &

sustains for 2 beats.

2. The quarter note

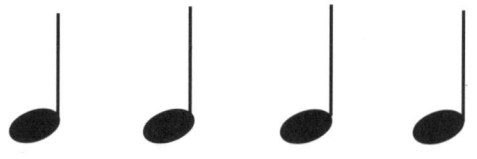

1 & 2 & 3 & 4 &

sustains for 1 beat, put another way, the quarter note is taken to be the beat

2. The eighth note
can be grouped in 2 or 4 with a (cross)beam or written individually

1 & 2 & 3 & 4 &

sustains for half a beat.

When counting time, the shortest, or fastest element always needs to be counted, understood and felt. The body movement should also be motivated by this sub-division of the beat.

practise counting

For all the rhythm elements to be arithmetically related there must be a beat that is kept at a constant speed or tempo. The ability to keep a tempo precise, once set, is valued highly - especially by the rest of the band. Please remember, it is not the drummers' total responsibility to keep time - you have to be EQUALLY responsible. A weak bass player, however good the drummer, will make the band sound terrible.

[DON'T LET IT BE YOU]

To help you control the tempo, learn to tap your foot on the beat. This will give you a focus for the beat that is independent of your fingers.

If you haven't got a metronome or drum machine (put one on your shopping list) and then look at your watch - 60 beats per minute is 1 beat per second.

As you watch the seconds tick by, synchronise your foot tap with them. Your foot is now tapping once every second or 60 B.P.M. And you can begin the exercises.

In addition try counting out loud: 1, 2, 3, 4, 1, 2, 3, 4 etc.., With each tap. Then try and divide the beat exactly into two by counting '&' between each number; 1 & 2 & 3 & 4 & etc. Keep the way you speak the count tight and percussive - you are learning rhythm, not talking.

Practise the following exercises regularly.

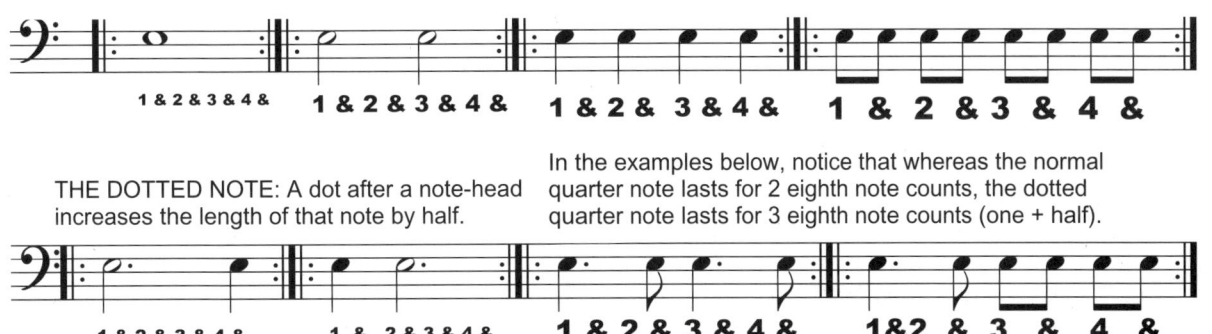

THE DOTTED NOTE: A dot after a note-head increases the length of that note by half.

In the examples below, notice that whereas the normal quarter note lasts for 2 eighth note counts, the dotted quarter note lasts for 3 eighth note counts (one + half).

THE TIE: ⌒ This symbol joins two note values together. In practise it means ignore the second of the two notes that are tied together. Watch out! this means the rhythm is going to be syncopated which requires good counting skills.

The power of silence

Silence plays a really important role in all music. As bass players, we can really create an impact if we know how to use silence.

The reason silence is so effective is that it provides contrast to sound. As bass is so powerful a sound, when silence is used in contrast, the effect is incredible.

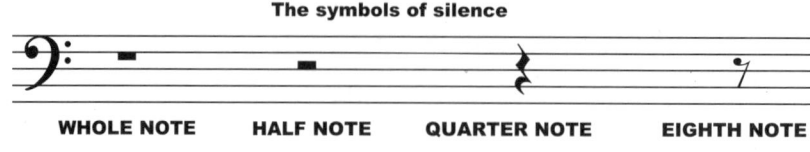

The following examples illustrate the importance of silence (notated by rest symbols) in music. You will also discover that allowing for silence in music, puts your counting ability to the test in a big way! Don' forget that you will need to stop the previous note from ringing (damp the string) by touching with the right hand or taking the pressure off the left hand finger.

The next examples are more difficult. The first is a very useful rhythm. By damping your notes on the 2nd and 4th beats - the snare drum will sound huge. For this illusion to work, your first note must run right up to the 2nd and 4th beats, i.e. there must be no gap between your note and the snare drum.

The one drawback to using silence is that it requires us to be even better musicians. Our control of the beat and counting needs to be total. You will find that the exercises on this page that incorporate silence, (called rests in music) are much harder than the previous exercises.

Don't cut corners when practising these exercises. If you are losing the beat, slow down a little and repeat. If you are still losing the beat, slow down even more and repeat and repeat.

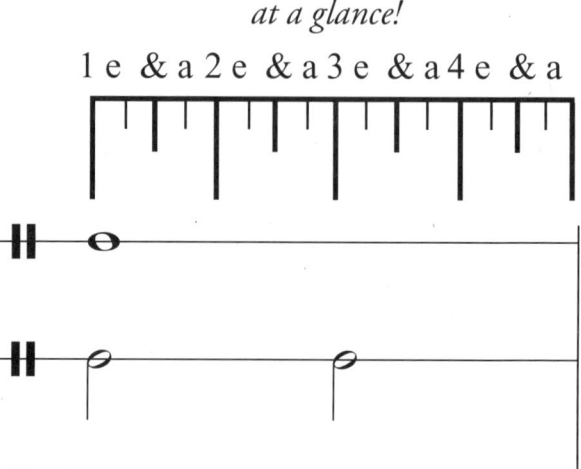

The arithmetic divisions of rhythm - at a glance!

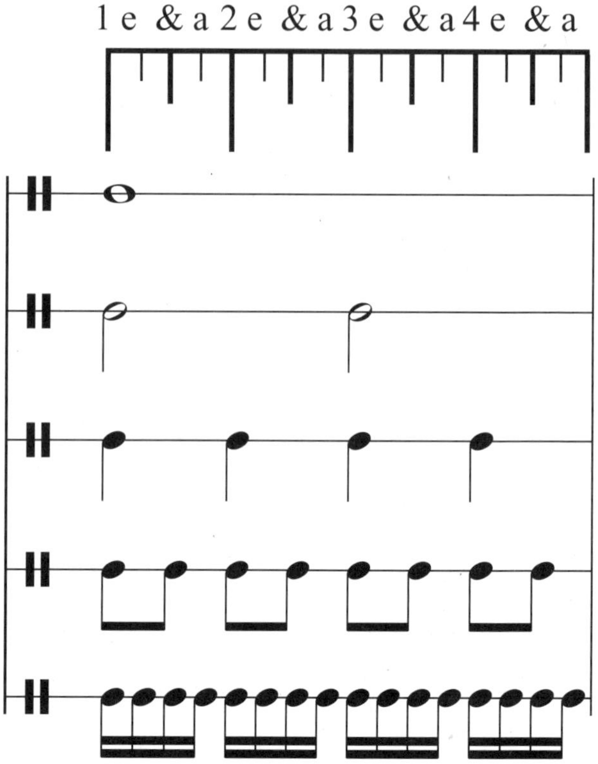

scales and keys

Earlier, when discussing the musical alphabet I mentioned that there are only seven letters of the alphabet required to describe music. However, by now you'll realise that the octave divides into 12 frets and therefore 12 notes. In nearly all types and styles of music the notes that make up the melody and harmony (chords) are derived from a set of seven notes only. The other five notes do not (usually) play a part.

These seven note sets are known as keys.

The result of playing all the notes of a key, in sequence, from the most important note (the key note or key centre) until this same note is reached at its octave, is known as a scale.

The word key, is usually used to describe and communicate which set of notes to play and a scale is all the notes of that 'set', played in sequence.

In music, there are different types of key (and scale) used by composers to create different moods and styles in music. The two most important types of key and scale are MAJOR and MINOR. In a simplistic way, the Major key is bright and positive and the Minor key is melancholy and sometimes plain miserable.

In addition to different types of key, composers may need to use different key centres, sometimes they may write a song in C major, which means the note C is revolved around and heard as the most important note. At other times a composer may use 'A major', which means the note 'A', is the most important.

There are a number of reasons why they might do this. The easiest reason to understand is; imagine two singers, one has a high voice and the other not quite so high. The song is originally written for a high voice. The singer with the 'not so high' voice has to lower the key - lower the important note, in order to be able to sing the higher notes of the song.

Whatever the reason for a song being in a particular key, the bad news is that you need to be prepared for any key to be used - yep! You have to learn them all.

The following examples show you how to play the major and minor scales.

Memorise the finger patterns and then practise starting the scales from a different note each time you practise them.

LEARN YOUR KEY SETS: KNOWN AS KEY SIGNATURES	
C MAJOR - All natural notes	C - D - E - F - G - A - B
G MAJOR - 1 sharp note	G - A - B - C - D - E - F♯
D MAJOR - 2 sharps	D - E - F♯ - G - A - B - C♯
A MAJOR - 3 sharps	A - B - C♯ - D - E - F♯ - G♯
E MAJOR - 4 sharps	E - F♯ - G♯ - A - B - C♯ - D♯
B MAJOR - 5 sharps	B - C♯ - D♯ - E - F♯ - G♯ - A♯
F♯ MAJOR - 6 sharps	F♯ - G♯ - A♯ - B - C♯ - D♯ - E♯
F MAJOR - 1 flat note	F - B - A - B♭ - C - D - E
B♭ MAJOR - 2 flats	B♭ - C - D - E♭ - F - G - A
E♭ MAJOR - 3 flats	E♭ - F - G - A♭ - B♭ - C - D
A♭ MAJOR - 4 flats	A♭ - B♭ - C - D♭ - E♭ - F - G
D♭ MAJOR - 5 flats	D♭ - E♭ - F - G♭ - A♭ B♭ - C
G♭ MAJOR - 6 flats	G♭ - A♭ - B♭ - C - D♭ - E♭ - F

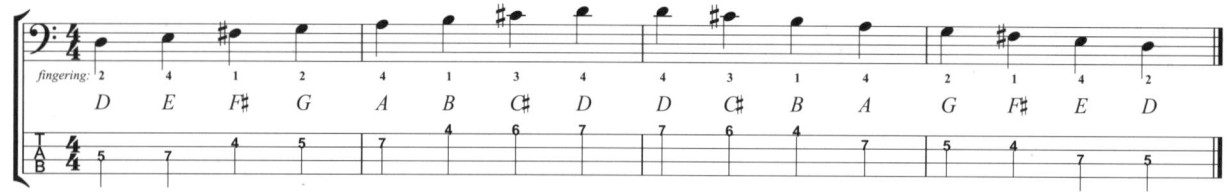

the major scale

Although the examples are in the key of D. When you have memorised the finger patterns, try playing the scales starting on any note found on either the 'E' string or the 'A' string.

Play each scale five or six times without pause and always try and make them sound musical. This is achieved by ensuring that the sound of each note sustains up to the next note.

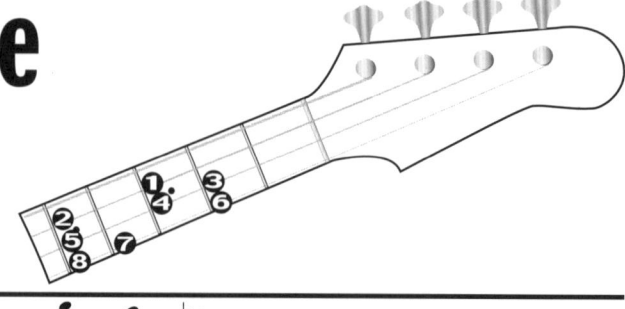

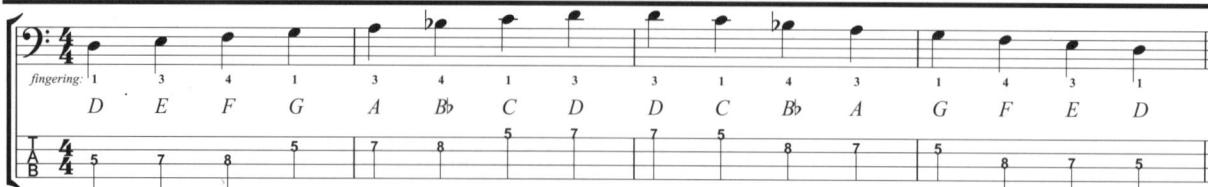

the minor scale

This scale is properly known as the 'natural minor scale'. It is used to create darker, more melancholy moods. By omitting the 2nd and 6th notes you create the next scale on this page - the pentatonic minor!

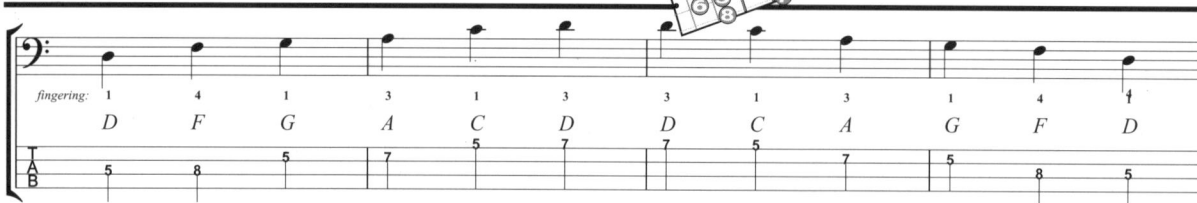

the pentatonic scale

The word 'pentatonic', means a five note scale. (The sixth note in the example is of course the octave, or 1st note repeated).

This is the most common scale in rock and blues etc.

Experiment a lot with this scale (in various keys) try and invent riffs and bass lines. You don't have to use all the notes of the scale to do this - two or three are often enough to create a riff.

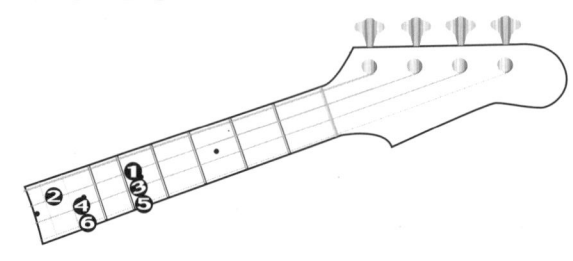

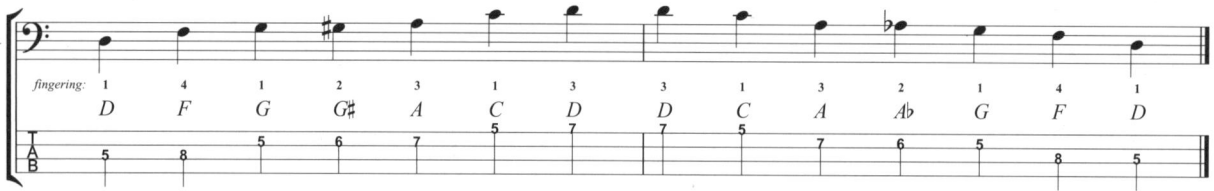

the blues scale

A blues scale is based on the pentatonic scale above. The fourth note, known usually as the flat five (or diminished 5th) is the note that creates the characteristic blues sound. Although this is a non-key tone. It can be used as a passing note, between two key tones (as in the scale) yet it also works when played from, or to. This creates a lot of 'bluesy' emotion.

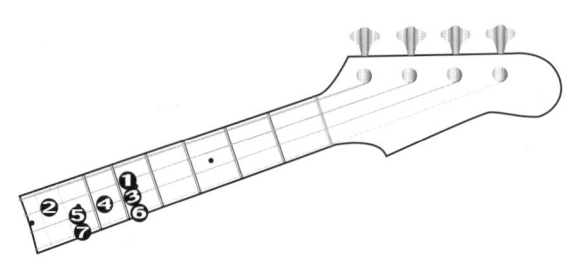

putting scales into practise

The Major Scale

The major scale tends to produce riffs that are bright and chirpy. Ex. 1 below has shades of a Calypso sound. Ex. 2 is a classic rock 'n roll type of riff.

The Minor Scale

The minor scale is good for creating moody riffs. Both the examples below use the third and sixth notes of the scale which are the notes that produce this effect!

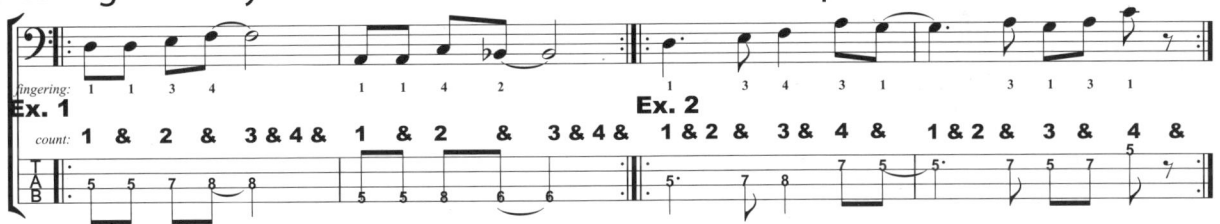

The Pentatonic Scale

The pentatonic scale will be the most familiar sounding scale. Easy to create riff after riff. The character is harder than minor - ideal for rock music generally!

The Blues Scale

These blues riffs, based on the blues scale, add to the scale in two ways. Very important in blues is to bend the 3rd of the (full minor) scale slightly (this is actually the second note of the blues scale - 'F' in the following examples). Bending the string means raising the pitch of the note slightly by dragging the string sideways. You don't have to bend far to get some blues emotion!

The second addition is the use of a chromatic (1 fret at a time) scale, ascending to the Key note - in the first example below this is C - F#- D.

Settling Down — Looking to the Future

groove and feel – your real priorities

Real bass playing is understanding how to achieve a good groove and a great feel.

The words 'groove' and 'feel' are thrown into every possible conversation discussing a bass players performance and ability.

So what is meant by these words? And how do you achieve a good groove?

The word groove is really an all embracing word used to describe the rhythm, dynamics, emotion and overall purpose of a musical part.

The difficulty players have in achieving a good groove is that it requires absolute consistency. The beat needs to be kept perfectly constant, the way in which you sub-divide the beat must be totally constant. Accents should be consistent with one another. If you play smoothly, that smoothness needs to be maintained throughout the song.

A good groove also depends on a musician being able to convey emotions. Whether this be sadness, aggression or excitement etc. the way in which you play the bass will transmit emotions.

Ultimately, it is essential that you truly feel and believe in, the emotions and ideas that you are trying to put across, while you are playing. To swap and change emotions and ideas from song to song is quite difficult to do genuinely.

Your aim as a bass player is to learn to control your emotions and thoughts in the same way that you learn to control your fingers and your understanding of music.

As you improve, you need to think less about how you play technically and more about how you play emotionally. It is a fact though, that if you are not in total control technically, you will not be able to concentrate enough on the music and emotions and will therefore struggle to play with feel and put across a great groove.

Technically feel is achieved by subtle variations in volume, tone, articulation (the exact length of a note) and timing.

The following examples: "Volume Control" and "Tone Control", suggest some ways that you can become aware of what to practise and what is possible.

VOLUME CONTROL (Dynamics Exercise)

On each string in turn, practise playing (using alternating fingers, or up and down strokes for the pick) as quietly as possible. Keep one note, and keep the rhythm constant eighth notes. Gradually increase the force of your playing, of course the volume will increase. Keep getting louder until you are playing much harder than normal, the bass may even buzz. Then, keeping the rhythm constant, gradually reduce volume until you get back to your quietest sound. The greater your dynamic range (difference between you loudest and softest notes) the better.

TONE CONTROL

There are two main ways to change the tone (apart from electronically, that is).
1. The angle and force of the finger as it strikes the string.
2. The distance from the bridge that you pluck the string.
To experiment with these ideas try one aspect at a time. Example 1; The 'A' string - 2 inches from the bridge - index finger only - constant rhythm while you vary the angle that the finger plucks the string. Start at your normal angel and push forward until you are plucking the string upwards, then gradually back, through normal, until your hand is almost flat on the bass. Or, example 2; the 'G' string - middle finger only - constant rhythm - start playing half an inch from the bridge and move slowly towards the neck. You'll notice in example 2 how the tone changes from bright and nasal to deep and warm. Invent variations on these examples.

how to get the most from listening to records

Watching and listening to other people is the way we learn to do most things. In music it is obvious and natural to listen to bands and musicians on the TV or radio and on record and try and emulate what they do.

You can approach the subject in a number of ways.

Most people start by trying to hear the bass lines in order to copy those lines. This is without doubt the place to start. Don't worry if you find it hard to pick out bass lines at first. As you learn and play more music your hearing will improve. Also your knowledge of what is likely to be being played will increase. Try and work out lines that are really clear.

The notes and rhythm of a bass line are to most people all that they listen for. This is a mistake. When you have the bass line worked out - listen again. How is the feel of the bass line being achieved. Copying a bass line to the extent of listening to the tone, the exact length of notes, dynamics etc. will reveal a great deal. You can learn more about the different styles of music by listening to these finer points, than you will learn by only taking notice of just notes and rhythm.

outline of composing bass lines

Writing your own bass lines is one of the most satisfying things you can do as a bass player. The subject of arrangement and composition can get very involved so the following are some simple principals to observe.

Write objectively; take note of the lyrics and the purpose of the song. A good bass line is one that fits the style and mood of the music.

Technical objectives; the song will be presented to you as a chord progression, melody and lyrics. There will also be obvious rhythmic stresses that need to be maintained.

As a bass player your role is actually quite complex. You provide the link between pure rhythm (drums) and the harmony (chords). In addition you can provide a link to the melody and indeed create melody either to work in conjunction with the main melody, or as individual counter melodies or even hooks (easily identified themes).

chords and how to deal with them

You need to understand how chords are constructed if you ever want to play more than root notes. A root note gives its name to the chord and is the starting point for the chord's construction. (E.g. 'A' is the root note of an 'A ' major chord.) Obviously you can create a bass line by playing the root notes only, combine with the same rhythm as the drummer's kick (bass) drum and you have a perfectly acceptable bass line. (Many recorded bass lines do no more!)

If, as is likely, you are a creative person, you will want the option of doing much more with your bass lines. To make this possible you need to know which notes make up the chords of the song. You also need to understand which set of seven notes (the key) results from the chord progression you are working to.

The Scale of C major

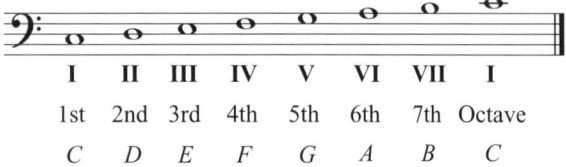

Chords are constructed by taking every other note of a scale and playing these notes at the same time. The most common chords only use three notes. These chords are known as triads and form the building blocks for all harmony or chord progressions.

To clarify their construction, take the note 'C'. If we call 'C' the root (beginning of chord) and take from the C major scale (C-D-E-F-G-A-B) every other note, (the 1st, 3rd and 5th notes), you get C - E - G. This is a chord of 'C' major. To work out any other major chord follow the same principal. Play the major scale from the root, and pick out the 3rd and 5th notes and add them to the root to create your triad.

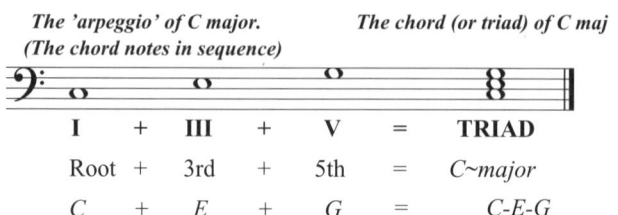

To construct a minor triad, use the same idea except use the minor scale to find the 3rd and 5th notes.

The next most common chord type is the '7' chord. The major 7 chord follows exactly the same idea as for the major triad, adding the 7th note to the root, 3rd and 5th. This, of course, results in a 4 note chord. The minor 7 chord again follows the idea except using the minor scale.

There is a 3rd type of '7' chord, which is most easily thought of as a mixture of major and minor. It is known properly as the 'dominant 7 chord', although most of us know is just play '7' (e.g. C7, G7 etc..). This chord is constructed by taking a MAJOR triad and adding the 7th from the minor scale (known as the minor 7th).

Chords are not difficult to learn or understand, the only problem with them is that there are so many to learn, so just take your time. Do try and memorise each new chord thoroughly when you come across one.

keys and how to recognise them

It is very helpful to know and understand the key (seven note set) that the music is using. Any melody you create will draw mainly from the key notes. In other words if you are in the key of 'C major', you will use only natural notes.

The key name will also tell you which note is the most important. There is a complete hierarchy of notes in a key. The key note is the most important, followed by the 5th note and the 4th note. (The relative importance of other notes is not all that significant.)

You can use notes from outside the key but these usually only work if they are placed between two notes that are in key. For example: if in C major you could always play a run back to 'C' that used; A - A♯ - B - C, because A♯ (the non-key tone) is between A and B, which are in key.

Keys are not all that obvious when you are presented with a chord progression. However, even if you are able to understand the notes that make up each chord, you don't want to be limited to just these notes. Melody ideas need to draw from all the notes in the key.

Key analysis can get quite involved, however as most music is quite straight forward the following method should prove quite effective in working out keys.

HOW TO ESTABLISH THE KEY FROM THE CHORD PROGRESSION

A typical chord progression: | Am | Am | G | F | Am | Dm | G7 | C ||

At first you will have no idea what key this is in. You need to be able to see which notes make up each chord and then the key will become clear.

Am	=	A	C	E
G	=	G	B	D
F	=	F	A	C
Dm	=	D	F	A
C	=	C	E	G

Run through all the notes found in all chords alphabetically to check that all seven letters are represented. It doesn't matter if they are sharp, flat or natural. However it is significant if you find two types using the same letter, e.g. F and F♯ as this indicates a key change. Key changes are quite common as changing the note set and / or the key centre causes a dramatic effect, making music more interesting.

The above example can quite quickly be seen to use only natural notes, there is no complication as all letters are represented and there are no contradictions of note name types (e.g. sharp and natural etc.). If you play (or get a friend to play) the chords you'll hear that the music resolves when it reaches C, meaning that C is the key centre and therefore gives its name to the key: C Major.

the 12 bar sequence

The 12 bar sequence or 12 bar blues is one of the commonest chord progressions in contemporary music.

It is very embarrassing not to know this progression as you will often be called on to jam (play without any preparation or rehearsal) with musicians you meet for the first time, using this progression.

It is useful also because it establishes the importance of the chords built on the 1st, 4th and 5th notes of the scale. Remember, on the previous page about keys, I told you that the key note (1st note or I) is the most important note, followed by the 5th and 4th notes (in that order). Chords built on these notes will sometimes be described as the I chord, the IV (4) chord and the V (5) chord. (Roman numerals are used if this is written down.)

These three chords all support and interact with one another to give the illusion that the 'I' chord is the strongest, or the place in the music where the sound is stable and at peace, or resolved.

Although these three chords are traditionally arranged in the order that we know as the 12 bar blues, they can be arranged in almost any order and structure to create an almost infinite number of compositions. Many songs use only these three

The 12 bar blues progression goes as follows - firstly with the chords written numerically

The 12 bar blues progression - in the key of G.

|| G | G | G | G | C | C | G | G | D | C | G | D ||

Really learn this progression well. It will sound familiar but commit it to memory none the less:

chords and are lovingly referred to as the 'three chord trick'. (Status Quo fans will immediately relate to this concept.)

Notice how the preceding riff is constructed. The notes in a G major chord are G - B - D (root, 3rd and 5th from the G major scale). The riff plays G (the root) twice, the 3rd twice and the 5th twice before concluding with a little melodic link to lead back to the root again. This principle of following the notes of the chord is adopted in all bass lines. A more creative line will try and disguise this simple principal a little better.

one bar repeating sequences

One of the most common devices for composing a bass line is to use one bar, or sometimes two bar sequences. These short sequences are usually known as riffs

When you invent a bass riff, it is usually quite simple to adapt this riff to fit the entire song. To some extent all bass lines will follow this idea.

When adapting riffs to fit onto a 12 bar blues (or other I-IV-V three chord trick composition) you need do no more than move your hand so that the riff starts on the root of the next chord. You should be able to play the riff with the same fingering exactly.

The following examples are all one bar riffs that can be easily adapted to fit a 12 bar blues in any key. Practise them all as 12 bar sons, repeating every 12 bars.

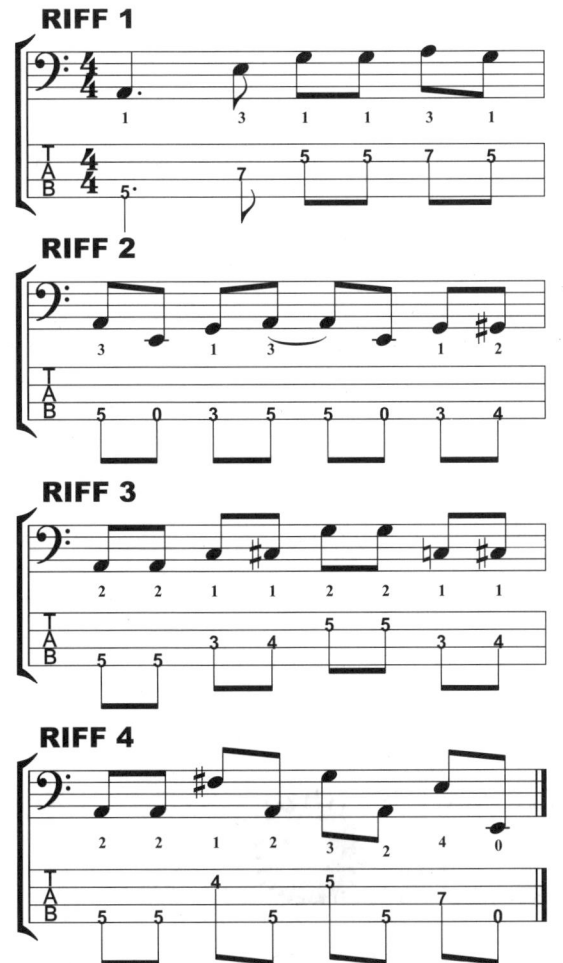
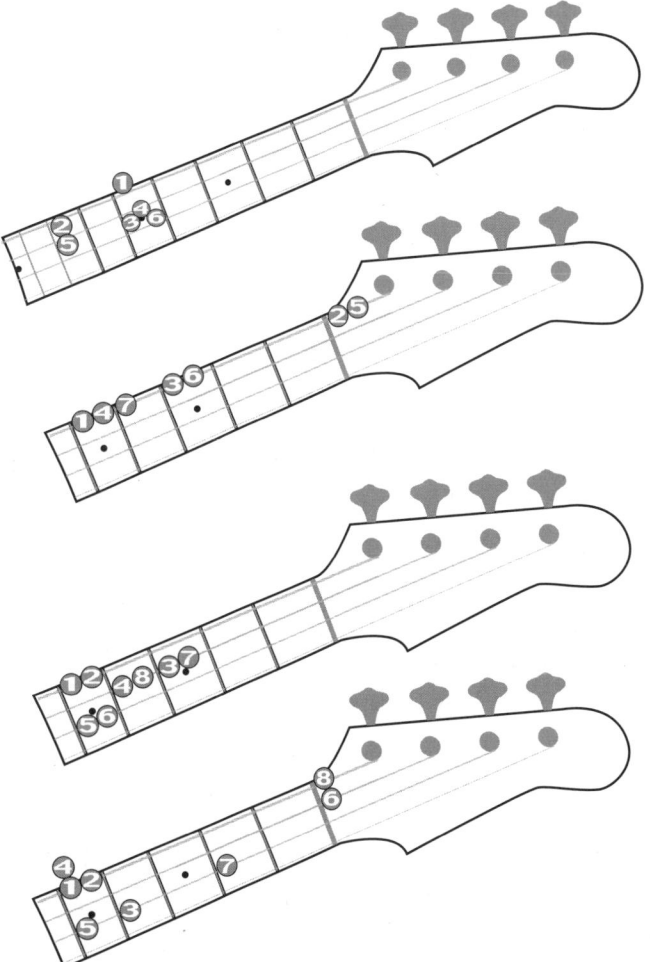

The Seven Week Itch
Getting Into A Band

know your fellow musicians

Eventually, you will need to set out, bass in hand to join your first band. You'll feel, if you have to audition, that all the pressure is on you. However, always turn this idea on its head and, believing in your abilities, use the audition to assess the potential of the band and the individual musicians that make it up. The following is a guide to what you can expect to find and what you should look for (and look out for and avoid - if possible).

the drummer

What do you call the guy that hangs around with musicians? Yes, your right hand man the drummer, the butt of most jokes However, as a bass player you must be fussy about the drummers you work with. Bad drummers will make you look bad - always.

Whilst it is true that your average drummer drinks to excess, smells like something between a brewery and a corpse and is generally the sort of person you'd cross the road to avoid, if he has the right priorities about his drumming you should accept his human failings gladly.

A drummer must be obsessed with playing TIME! (So should you.) Avoid drummers who don't know what a metronome is, or whose timing is clearly suspect.

If they spend the entire rehearsal practising ridiculous fills and tom tom rolls, yet can't keep the beat with accuracy and consistency - walk away, you don't need it.

the guitarist

What a pain in the arse. Guitarists - who needs them. Well unfortunately you do. Some guitarists reckon they're pure lead players or pure rhythm. Personally I'm very suspicious of this. I like guitarists that know how to play their instrument properly which means both lead and rhythm.

If you can find a guitarist that can fit into a band, arrange his parts sympathetically and objectively - buy him, never leave his side.

the vocalist

If you're worried about guitarists then bear in mind they're angels compared to vocalists. The earlier joke about drummers is equally at home with your average vocalist.

If you take into account that somewhere beneath the dyed, diseased birds nest called a hair style, there's a birth mark looking to you and me like three sixes, you should be able to get along fine with vocalists.

The reality is an ego maniac, obsessed by expensive effects units and high volume. Usually he doesn't know what chord he's playing or why, nor how to communicate what he's playing!

The best thing to hope for with a vocalist is that they sound different. If they can actually sing as well, then you've found your man (or woman, of course).

the keyboard player

Keyboard players come in two forms. The synth player and the piano player.

The synth player hasn't a clue what he's doing, but has pots of cash so can always find a band. His speciality is buying the latest hi-tech kit and making silly noises - if you're lucky he'll create some wonderful atmospheres.

The piano player on the other hand either has, or will claim to have, a diploma in music - will have been to some hoity-toity music college and will by now have a hideous beard.

He will know everything about music - well he'll know more than anyone else and so gets away with the pretence.

the sax player

If you ask any sax player what style he plays they'll always say, in an affected husky, gin soaked voice - Jazz, I play mainly jazz man".

Beware, this doesn't necessarily mean they can actually play jazz, or even know what it is - but they've learned that other musicians are impressed by this line and so use it all the time.

the diplomatic bass player

Making music is a very personal and emotional experience. This is why it can be very difficult to get a whole band to agree on anything from direction to specific musical ideas.

To get on with your fellow musicians you need to be quite a diplomat. Always put the needs of the song first. Be objective; does the idea being argued about suit the song.

Try not to dismiss other people's ideas out of hand, even if they're trying to tell you how to play your instrument.

Just occasionally, they may have a good point, so get into the habit of listening to other people's ideas and points of view. You usually get musicians moaning about your bass part if it is causing them difficulty in putting their part across. The may not express it like this for fear of exposing their own weaknesses. However, their opinion does affect the song and band as a whole - so try and listen and compromise if possible.

writing a bass line

Hopefully you now have a fairly good idea how to work out the notes in chords. In addition to this you should be able to establish the note set or key of the chord progression and spot any key changes.

When you are presented with a song by you new band you will, if you're lucky, get the chords scribbled down on a scrap of paper.

If possible, try and spend a little time writing the song out neatly. Try and write the format or structure of the song out at the top e.g.:
    INTRO
    VERSE 1
    VERSE 2
    CHORUS   etc.

Next, work out the notes in all of the chords and from these establish the key or keys that the music is in.

You should then always observe a little common sense. The notes found in the chord are the most important notes to use. The root in particular should be played as your principal note. Try if possible to include another note from the chord in a prominent position in the bar to ensure that you're providing a correct accompaniment.

Next, listen to the drummer. His kick (bass) drum will be illustrating the main accents in the groove of the song. You don't necessarily have to play every time the kick drum is played and you are not restricted to only playing when the kick plays. However, you must know what the kick is doing to make best use of it and it should always be your rhythmic guide. The hi-hat is also important as it illustrates how the beat is sub-dividing.

When you have understood your responsibilities to the harmony (chords) and rhythm you can try and craft melody onto the part. Notes that are in the key but outside the chord can be used in two main ways.

1. As passing or linking notes between two notes found in the chord. E.g.; if the chord is G major and you begin by playing the root (G) you could next play 'A' and then 'B'. The 'A' is now heard as a melodic passing note between the root (G) and the 3rd (B). The advantage of using non-chord tones in this way is that you can do it as much as you like without weakening the chord or changing it's character.

2. A non-chord tone can be used in a position of prominence, or held for a long time or accented in the way you would normally reserve for your main chord tones. Some great effects and tensions can be achieved by doing this, however it can really only be done once in any bar as it will have an impact on the character of the chord.

outline of improvisation

Improvisation is a spontaneous composition. It is not achieved by luck but by good musicians with a lot of knowledge and / or experience.

When improvising, all notes that you play should be understood before you play them. You should know what notes are and what role they will play in the music.

You can start off by giving an illusion of improvisation by writing slightly different versions of your bass line and mixing them up. If you can do this objectively, i.e. place the right variation with the right top line then this can be very effective.

You can also invent a variety of fills (linking and building passages usually used to link song sections [verse to chorus etc.]). By varying these fills you can give everyone the impression that you are improvising, so long as you are using your invention objectively to keep a song alive.

Top bass players have the experience, ability and thorough knowledge of their instrument to give life to a bass line by subtle adjustments to the principal line. They can invent fills on the spot to suit the moment. They can genuinely 'hear' their improvisations before they play them. They know that what they play will make sense compositionally.

Although in a book like this I can only give you a brief insight into improvisation, you can take steps to prepare yourself by trying to learn everything VERY thoroughly. FINGERBOARD, CHORDS AND KEYS IN PARTICULAR.

writing bass lines - examples

The following should be a guide as to how a bass line is put together.

Example 1:

Main points to note:

Chord Progression: || Em | Em | Am | B7 ||
Chord notes   Em = E-G-B
                   Am = A-C-E
                   B7 = B-D#-F#-A

1. Rhythm idea (concept) repeats every bar.
2. Main riff + Root, 3rd, octave.
3. 3rd bar modified = Root, 2nd note of scale acting as passing note to: 3rd of chord.
4. Final bar: root, 7th (in this case found a tone below the root) root, adds to original rhythm concept when it links back to the beginning with a simple descending scale (fill).

Example 2:

Chord Progression: || Dm7 | Em7 | G7 | C ||
Chord notes   Dm7 = D-F-A-C
                   Em7 = E-G-B-D
                 G7 = G-B-D-F
                 C = C-E-G

1. Rhythm concept one bar - repeating
2. Bars 1 & 2: root, (descend to) 5th, 7th root, rpt.....
3. Root, 5th, 6th; used to keep shape and reference to previous chord.

improvisation and fill examples

Improvisation is achieved with a lot of knowledge and experience. The knowledge can be slowly and steadily gained. The principal area of knowledge required is total fingerboard knowledge allied with knowledge of chords and keys. You have to gradually acquire knowledge of the make-up of all chords.

The example shows 5 permutations of a G major triad. There are many more permutations and if you really know your fingerboard you will easily find them.

An excellent practise routine is to use a 12 bar blues progression as a base and practise all possible permutations of all three chords within a definite structure - this means to time: a metronome, drum machine or tape of the chords.

A further area of investigation that will enable you to improvise to a certain extent, is the ability to create fills 'off the cuff'.

A fill is really a phrase that links one section of a song to another, and usually this means one chord to another (different) chord.

The commonest approach to fills is to employ scales.

Example 1: The chords to be linked are G major to C major. There is a simple chromatic scale used (a chromatic scale is a scale made up of semitones - 1 fret intervals). In this example the last four notes are chromatic.

Example 2: The chords once again are G to C, this time there is a descending major scale (C major) in use.

Example 3: The chords are D7 to C7, the 5th of the D7 chord is deliberately chosen as the 2nd note, from here it links chromatically to C.

Example 4: D7 to G7; this fill uses the two strongest 'set up' notes, rather than a scale. The 5th of the current chord as the 2nd note, then back to the root - this root will now be heard as the 5th of the next chord, so creating expectation. The final note being a semitone below the G. This note is called the leading tone and is a very strong linking note, as the listener hears it as establishing the key note - in this case G.

SHOWING OFF
THE ART OF PERFORMANCE

the paying public

Whatever you ambition, there will come a time when you want to get out and perform live. It will help if you appreciate that you perform to entertain the public. If you're performing for yourself then there's something wrong.

Although this may sound obvious, the point is that good performance depends upon having the right attitude.

Whether an audience appears to be enjoying the gig or not, should not affect the way you and the band perform. Treat the audience with respect and play to them for their benefit. Also don't try and bully them into participation (especially if there are only a few people there propping up the bar).

Results will come if you project yourself to an audience and are obviously there for their enjoyment rather than some self-indulgence on your part.

eye to eye

Use your eyes to good effect when performing. Learn to look out to the audience, not at your instrument. Don't actually 'eyeball' anyone - pick 2 or 3 points on the back wall and focus on them. This gives the impression that you are playing to the audience.

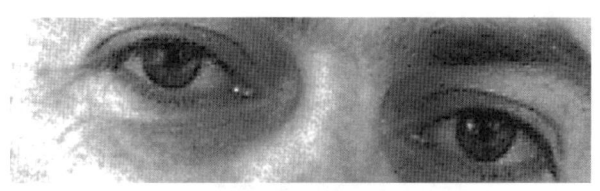

It's worth practising the 'technique' of looking at points while you rehearse your bass lines. If your eyes look confident, then even if you're nervous, you'll come across as a confident performer.

gigging

Keep the bass lines you intend to perform well within your limits. Gigs tend to throw up problems that you wouldn't believe. For example you may not be able to hear yourself, hear the vocals or even the drums. Things always go wrong with the equipment. This can usually be fixed, but you may have missed your chance to sound-check as a result. Panic may set in, or you may be rushed - all these pressures can take their toll, especially if your bass lines are over ambitious.

Get into the habit of keeping spares and packing them for every gig! Spare strings (vital), spare lead (preferably 2), spare mains lead. In addition, a basic tool kit; screwdriver set (to fit guitar fittings and plugs and amps), soldering iron (don't forget the solder) plenty of spare picks - if you play this style. A roll of gaffer tape will always be useful!

Be aware of security! Never leave your valuable equipment unguarded for a second.

recording

The best quick tip for recording is: BE PREPARED before you go into the studio. Studio time, at any level, is expensive. Know what sound you want, know your part thoroughly (e.g. without vocals to guide you etc.). Get a good sound at source, never be fobbed off with a "we'll sort it out later in the mix", from the engineer.

Never stop if you make a mistake, you may interrupt the perfect drum take. Even if you do make a mistake, you can 'drop in' or go over the error later - so don't worry about the odd mistake. Having said that, the feel of a bass line is all about consistency and continuity, so it is preferable to record a line all the way through- at least aim to achieve this!

slap style – bring the bass up front!

A great way to show off is to learn the slap style. Seriously, you need to use the style carefully as other

musicians get worried when the bass player starts to slap. It can though, bring the bass to the front and be incredibly dynamic. Obviously, a whole book could be devoted to this style but here are the main points with photos.

Slap = striking the string with the thumb. Position your arm as in the photo. The thumb should hover over the last fret, about an inch from the string. With a single movement that is totally loose and relaxed, whip the thumb out to 90 degrees and before it stops, whip it back onto the string.

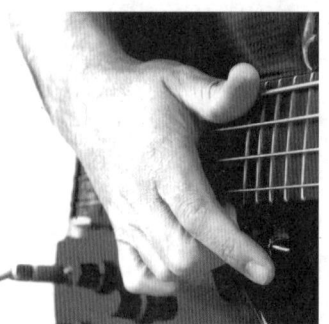

Pop = pluck (usually the G & D strings) by lifting vertically (not too far) and then releasing with a snap - the string will race back onto the fretboard, to give that unmistakable twang!

Are You Serious? Some Stuff To Keep You Going

In this final chapter, I'm going to leave you with a few riffs, additional technique and rhythm exercises and a mega riff for the slap bass style.

Nothing in this chapter is likely to be very easy for total beginners.

Learn at a slow tempo. Work out the rhythm first (bar by bar if necessary). Ensure that you are counting and tapping your foot correctly. Then work out the notes and where to play them, finally put rhythm and notes together. Be methodical and patient and you'll soon be able to play these lines.

1. This first bass line is not too hard to play - the rhythm is all quarter notes. The main points to note are that the riff begins with the root of the chord, moves to the third and then links to the next root chromatically. You can use this method to create your own, similar bass lines with different chord progressions.

2. Bass line 2 uses octaves, alternating between a low note and a middle note octave. Octaves are very useful to the bass player. An octave bass line has considerable energy and yet is very easy to compose. All you need to do is follow the root note for each chord, fit your hand into an octave shape (1st finger on low note, 4th finger two frets towards you on the next but one string) and alternate in a tasteful manner. The following bass line is not too hard although the off-beat stress on the '3 and', needs controlled counting.

The left hand will be quite busy, as it will have to move around in a sort of block shape for each new chord. It can be effective to keep the index finger of the right hand for low octave notes and the middle finger for mid octave notes.

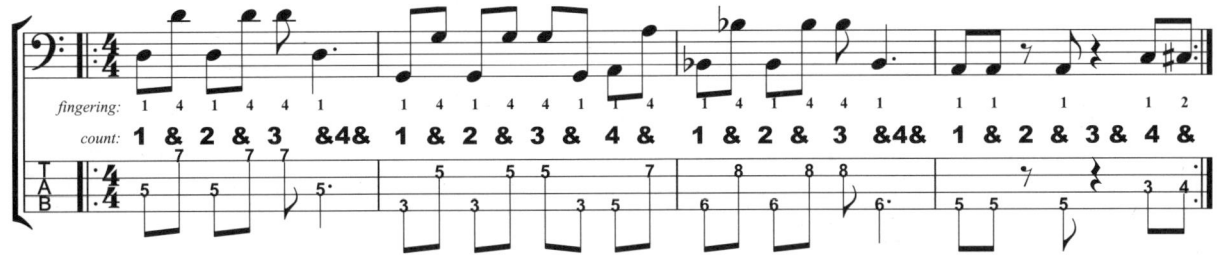

3. The next bass line has lots of rests (silence) and lots of notes played off the beat (syncopation). If you're going to play this line convincingly, your foot tap should remain in control tapping only on the beat. To get the subdivision of the beat correct, count out loud strongly and evenly. Time-keeping is everything on this riff. As you practise try and ignore minor note errors - always keep moving, keep in time,

Notice how open strings are used to help change position!

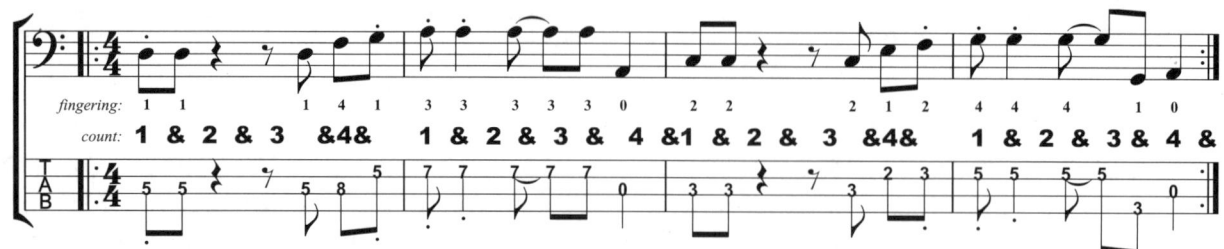

triple time – *12th notes*

Up till now you have only had to deal with 1) whole notes, 2) half notes 3) quarter notes and 4) eighth notes. The eighth notes meant; divide the beat into 2 equal parts. However, rhythm needs to be much more flexible than this. The beat can divide into 3 equal parts - triplets, 4 equal parts - sixteenth notes. If you want to get really carried away - you can have musical beats dividing into five, six seven or eight equal parts - in fact any subdivision of the beat is possible.

The following bass line is built around a rhythm know as the shuffle. When playing triple time grooves, always stress the note on the beat, so that it is actually slightly longer than the following 2 notes. (Say the word "following" and you'll naturally stress the "foll" syllable which makes it slightly longer than the "ow" and "ing" syllables.

sixteenth note introduction

Sixteenth notes greatly increase your rhythmic and musical potential. With this increase in creative possibility comes a considerable increase in difficulty.

When beginning to learn about sixteenth notes your first goal should be to understand how to divide the beat into four equal parts. Do this by counting: **1 & 2 & 3 & 4 &**

Practise the following exercises, which illustrate the most commonly used patterns.

When playing patterns or grooves that contain mixtures of sixteenth notes and other elements (eighth notes, quarter notes etc.) always keep the sixteenth note count (1 e & a etc.) going. This will ensure that you play accurately and most important will maintain the consistency of the groove.

slap style – serious riff

I'm not going to pretend that you will completely understand this style of playing from a couple of brief paragraphs. However, there's no reason why you can't have a bit of fun trying!

The slap style consists of:
    1. The thumb striking the strings (most commonly the E & A strings) = 'the slap'.
    2. The index and / or middle finger plucking (upwards) on the D & G strings (mainly) = 'the pop'.
    3. The "dead" (or choked or muted) note - where the left hand damps the strings so that when struck by either the thumb or finger there is only a percussive thud.

    4. The "hammer-on"; where the right thumb or finger plays once only and the left hand finger hammers onto a new note (usually one or two frets above the first note).
    5. The "lift-off"; a kind of reverse of the hammer-on, to make it work you actually have to pluck the string with the finger of the left hand as it leaves the string
    6. Left hand percussive technique - the most advanced of the techniques where the left hand 'hits' the string, usually in between a barrage of thumb slaps and pops.

Try and decipher the riff below - learn slowly, even if it sounds awful slow, gradually speeding up as you get the hang of it all.

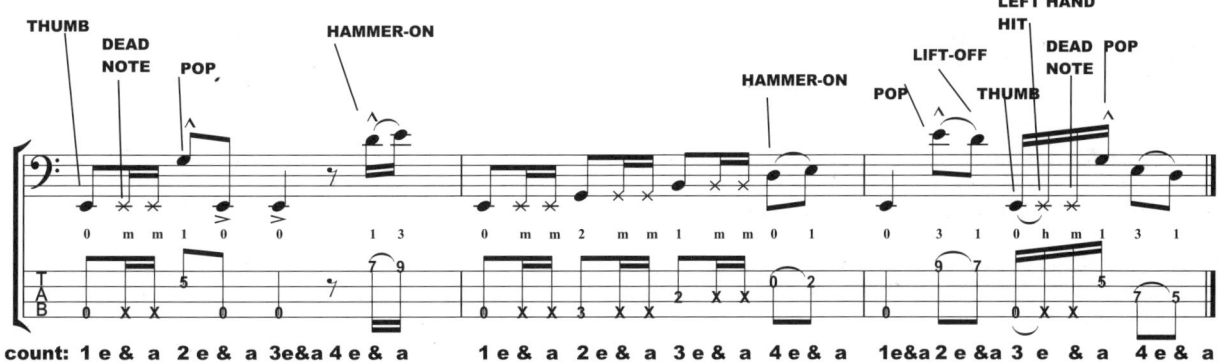

additional technique exercises

your worst nightmare!
4-3-2-1, 1-2-3-4 exercise,
across strings -ouch!

One note on each. This is not easy, so go slowly at first and keep the finger shape correct.

String crossing is especially tricky for the right hand - so really study the right hand when practising this one.

major scale in thirds

As with all scale exercises try and keep the sound smooth and joined up. Make sure the shape of the hand is maintained as you go backwards and forwards through this exercise.

You can also reverse the procedure for a descending scale in thirds and you can, of course, apply the idea to any type of scale.

octave exercises

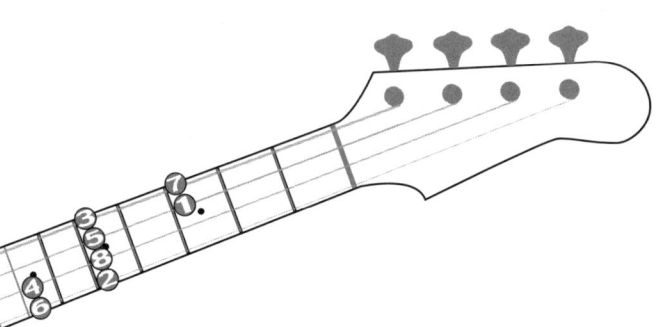

Octave technique: The right hand usually plays the low note with the index finger and the octave with the middle finger. This is often the case even if there are two low notes repeated.

Left hand technique: Octaves are nearly always played using the first finger on the low note and the fourth Finger on the octave.

notes:

Bass guitar
Bass guitar
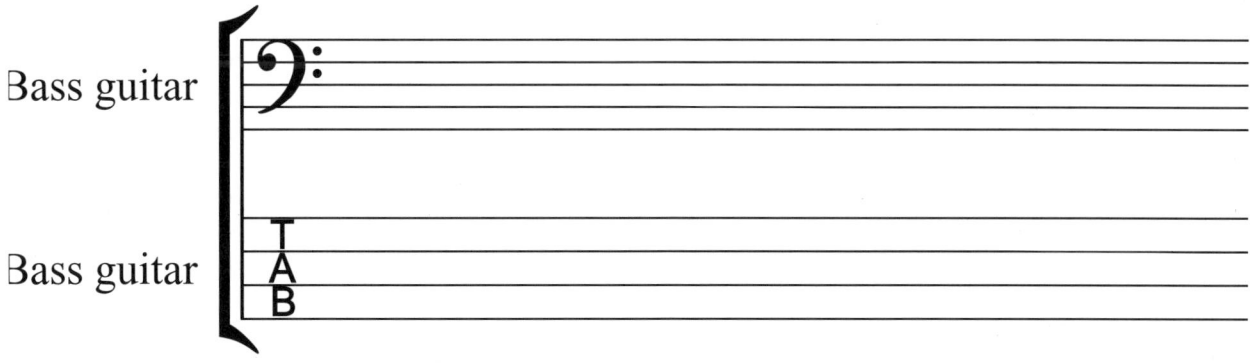

notes:

Bass guitar
Bass guitar